Blessings for Dogs

Amy Hunt

Illustrated by Marian Nixon

Illustrations © 2005 by Marian Nixon
Book design by Maura Fadden Rosenthal / Mspace

ISBN-13: 978-0-7407-4161-6

ISBN-10: 0-7407-4161-6

Library of Congress Control Number: 2005921768

Introduction

Affectionate and steadfast, dogs have been an integral part of our lives for thousands of years. In earlier days, canines earned their keep by providing protection and help with hunting, as well as friendship. While times have changed, we continue, up to this day, to rely on dogs for security and companionship.

At times, as you will read, dogs prove their intelligence and bravery by performing astounding rescues and almost miraculous feats. But most of the time, they are simply our good friends—and the most loyal companions we could ever hope for. We are privileged to enjoy their sweet, joyful natures and to accept their unconditional love. Simply put, dogs are blessings in our lives. This book celebrates and pays tribute to dogs by offering them our heartfelt blessings through words of love, admiration, and appreciation for all that they do.

Bless you
   for greeting me
as if I've been gone
   for a year
every time
   I come in the door.

May you always love me
as much as you love
the sound
of the can opener.

Bless you,
my clever canine,
for being so smart.

I LOVE THE WAY YOU ENJOY
THE SIMPLE THINGS IN LIFE,
LIKE AN OPEN WINDOW DURING
A CAR RIDE.

Bless you
    for pretending to be ferocious
when you bark at strangers
    who come to the door.

Bless you for being
the kind of friend
who doesn't need
a lot of conversation.

Greyfriars Bobby

One of the most photographed statues in all of Scotland is that of a simple bronze dog.

The dog's name was Bobby, a Skye terrier who served as a watchdog for Edinburgh police officer John Gray. In 1858, Constable Gray died and was buried in the Greyfriars Kirk churchyard. Sadly, his grave was untended; few mourners came to visit, with the exception of one, his dedicated and loyal dog, Bobby. Animals were not allowed on the cemetery grounds, and Bobby was repeatedly and firmly sent away. However, he always came right back. In time, Bobby won the admiration of the cemetery's gardener, James Brown. For fourteen long years, this devoted dog was allowed access to the cemetery and kept a continual watch over his master's

grave. Bobby soon became a local legend. He was granted the freedom to roam the town unattended until he died, in 1872. This loyal dog was then buried next to his master at Greyfriars. Today, a statue stands near the crest of Candlemaker Row, at the entrance of the churchyard gates, offering testimony to the silent blessing of a dog and his master.

Bless you
    for performing
on command when
    I want to show you
off to my friends.

May you always
    do your job
of serving as a
    canine garbage disposal.

Bless you
    for letting me
nap on the couch
    while you sleep on the floor—
at least once in a while.

Bless you
    for making me
exercise
        on those long walks.

I LOVE THE WAY YOU ACT SO GOOFY AND SCARED OF THE SOUND OF BARKING ON THE TV.

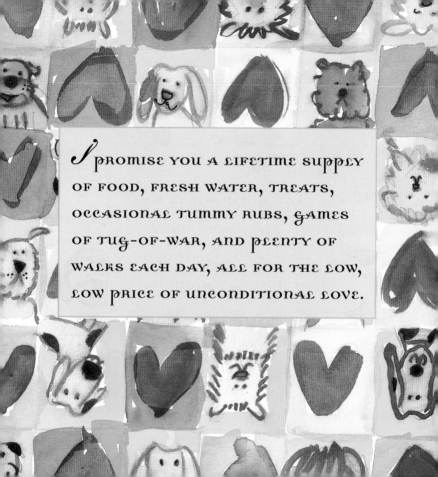

I PROMISE YOU A LIFETIME SUPPLY OF FOOD, FRESH WATER, TREATS, OCCASIONAL TUMMY RUBS, GAMES OF TUG-OF-WAR, AND PLENTY OF WALKS EACH DAY, ALL FOR THE LOW, LOW PRICE OF UNCONDITIONAL LOVE.

Bless you
    for not hating me
when you come back
    from the groomer
with bows in your hair.

Bless you
for loving me
unconditionally.

Bless you
    for letting me
sleep in
    a few times a year.

Bless you
  for believing you're
part of the family
  even if you're the only one
with fur and a tail.

Happily Ever After

Frisbee was a beautiful collie belonging to Doug Preston. One day, Frisbee disappeared. Doug was heartbroken. He put up flyers and called all the nearby shelters, hoping to find him.

A month later, one of the shelters called to say that a collie matching Frisbee's description had been brought in. Doug raced over, only to find that the dog was not his cherished friend. But Doug decided to honor Frisbee's memory by reaching out to another lost stray dog, and he took the collie home with him.

Fifteen miles away, Kelly Jordan had also lost a collie. When her local shelter called to say they had taken in a stray collie, she hurried to the shelter but discovered that

the dog was not Laddie. However, she was so taken with this collie that she decided to adopt him. While she was filling out the adoption papers, Doug Preston walked into the shelter. He had also heard about the collie at the shelter, and he was still hoping to find Frisbee.

Right away, Doug saw that the collie was indeed Frisbee! Kelly, of course, was happy to see Frisbee reunited with his owner. Doug explained to Kelly about adopting the collie he found at the other shelter. When Kelly saw the dog in his truck, she realized that it was her own long-lost Laddie! The miraculous reunion was complete when Doug and Kelly married a year later. These matchmaking dogs proved to be a true blessing in the lives of Doug and Kelly!

Bless you
   for not scaring
the mailperson . . .
   too much!

May you never
be able
to spell the word
V-E-T.

Don't ever lose
your beautiful
doggy smile.

Bless you
for not hating me
when I have to give you
a bath.

Bless you
for bringing me
attention when we
go to the park.

I AM GRATEFUL THAT YOU CONTINUE TO FALL FOR THE "You're going to get a cookie" TRICK EVERY TIME I HAVE TO DISTRACT YOU FROM SOMETHING.

May you always forgive me
when I yell about
your muddy paw prints
on the kitchen floor.

Bless you
   for not hurting me
when I have to
   brush your teeth.

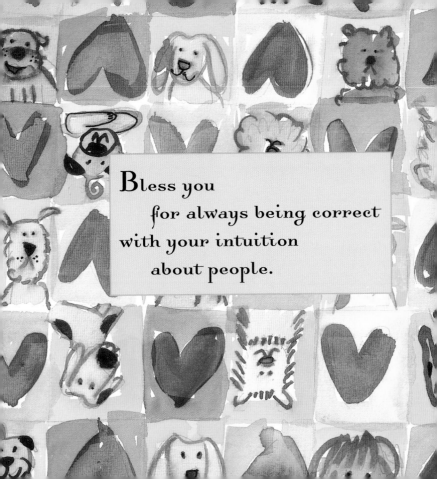

Bless you
     for always being correct
with your intuition
     about people.

*S*OMEHOW YOU ALWAYS KNOW WHEN
I NEED YOU TO BE INTIMIDATING AND
WHEN I NEED YOU TO BE CUTE AND
CUDDLY.

Bless you
for knowing
when you've done
something bad.

Bless you
for asking for
forgiveness.

Helen, the Deaf Dalmatian

Helen was a beautiful spotted dalmatian puppy. Unfortunately, she was born deaf, and her owner was not able to find a home for her. He took her to the local vet, requesting that she be put to sleep.

Lydia Martinez was working as a receptionist at the veterinary office when the puppy was brought in. Instantly taken with the pup, she decided to adopt her. Lydia brought Helen home to her husband, Tony, and her daughter, Anna, who quickly fell in love with her.

One evening, Lydia and Tony were awakened by Helen's frantic cries. When Helen took Lydia's hand in her mouth and attempted to pull her out of the room, Lydia and Tony understood that Helen wanted them to follow her. They

raced with Helen into the hall and were met by thick smoke. Their smoke alarm had somehow failed and the house was on fire! Thanks to Helen, the entire Martinez family escaped unharmed. The dalmatian had truly served as a blessing in their lives.

Bless you
    for letting me
pretend you're
    a dog-show winner.

Bless you
   for not chewing
on my favorite shoes
   (except that one time).

May you always keep
your kind and
gentle heart.

I LOVE THE WAY YOU GET THAT HOPEFUL LOOK IN YOUR EYES EVERY TIME THE REFRIGERATOR DOOR OPENS.

Bless you
   for letting me
 hog all the blankets
      at night.

Bless you
 for not being insulted
when I wash my face
 after you've kissed it.

I PROMISE NEVER TO FORGET WHAT YOU TAUGHT ME—TO HAVE A HEART THAT IS AS ABSOLUTELY LOVING AND LOYAL AS YOURS.

I appreciate—I really do—your gift of a damp and half-chewed dog bone, even if I don't always show it.

Angel

It was 1941 in war-torn France, and fourteen-year-old Esther Cohen was completely alone in the world. Hours before, her previously happy family had been huddled in the street where she had once played with her friends. Now, the street held the bloody horror of murder; her parents and baby brother were among the slaughtered. Unnoticed, Esther ran from the scene as fast as she could. Farther and farther she ran until she entered a dense forest, where she collapsed from exhaustion and terror.

She awoke with a jolt to discover a large scruffy dog of unknown breed licking her face! Where had he come from? Esther welcomed the dog's friendly presence and named him Angel.

For the remainder of the war, Esther and Angel remained hidden in the forest. Struggling to survive any way they could, they formed an unbreakable bond. When the war ended and Esther was able to return to a more normal life (bringing Angel with her, of course), she would often tell the story of her dog and how he had been her saving grace. "He was my friend and he gave me the will and strength to go on," she would explain. "He was all I had. He saved my life."

Bless you,
my canine friend,
for being true and loyal.

Bless you
      for letting me
eat my lunch
      when you really expected
to eat it yourself.

Bless you
 for acting like
you think you're
 a person.

Bless you
   for understanding
when I'm too tired
   to take you for
a long walk.

I AM REALLY SORRY THAT I GOT SO MAD WHEN YOU KNOCKED ALL THE BREAKABLES OFF THE COFFEE TABLE WITH YOUR HAPPY, WAGGING TAIL.

Bless you
    for being silly
like a goofy clown
    when I need to laugh.

May you always keep
your delightful
doggy sense of humor.

Bless you
   for trusting me
to take care of you.

Bless you
    for always
wanting to hang out with me,
    even if we sit in silence.

Bless you
for not only
being man's best friend
but for being *my* best friend!